W9-AUK-367

No part of this book may be reproduced or transmitted in any form

or by any means, graphic, electronic, or mechanical, including

photocopying, recording, taping, or by any information storage

retrieval system, without the permission, in writing, from the

publisher.

Parent Forward

My son, AJ, and I wrote the book we wish we would have had to read many years ago, when we were struggling through the frustrations of his learning challenges, ultimately diagnosed as dyslexia. Without any known family history of dyslexia, we were unaware of what symptoms to look for, or even recognize. We only knew frustration and confusion pre-diagnosis, and the overwhelming feeling of 'now what?' when we received the confirmation that AJ was indeed dyslexic. While there are many reference books out there written about dyslexia and learning differences by learned PhDs, this is simply a book written for children and their parents from the child's perspective. It is our story of early despair, followed by hope and pride, and confidence and resilience. We want to share our experience with all the other families dealing with the struggle of learning differences, difficulties, and disabilities. We want to replace any frustration, shame, or despondency with the comfort of knowing that these are marvelously interesting brains that come with many gifts. It is important to know that there are many educational resources and tools, several avenues for help, and many paths to learning. Read on!

Laurie

Laurie and AJ live in Marin County in Northern California. Laurie works for a non-profit and dedicates her free time to children's advocacy issues. AJ is now in Middle School, getting straight A's, and loves photography and sailing.

Why Can't I Read?

On a scale of one to ten, I'd say I enjoyed reading in school about a negative five.

Negative five? Why, you ask?

Because I couldn't read, and school is all about reading.

I'd try hard. I really would. But those words on the page made no sense to me. I could see letters just fine, but sounding out letters to form words was too hard for me.

If you're like me, someone else is even reading this book to you right now.

Everyone knows I'm smart—even really smart—but no one could understand why I couldn't read better.

"How could this boy who is so smart, so clever . . . not read?! He must not be trying." Or, "It's a developmental lag." That means that I'll be able to read when I get a little older.

If I heard "you need to try harder," or "it will click one day," or "you're just not motivated to read," one more time, I thought I might scream!

I was trying hard, and I REALLY wanted to learn to read.
But NOTHING was clicking in my head.

Forget spelling. I could work hard all week and still have no idea how to spell any words on my spelling test on Friday.

You see, I can't remember spelling patterns. Every time I read a spelling word is like seeing it for the first time-even repeated on the same page.

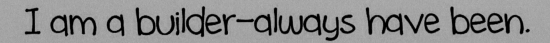

I am a builder-always have been.

I've invented really
cool stuff, like a projector,
an air pressurized dart gun,
a fan, a greenhouse, and a lamp.

I built a sailboat and go-kart all by myself.
It was easier to create my inventions than
it was to memorize how to spell a simple
word like 'was.' I still want to spell it 'woz.'

Reading was just too hard.
I would feel frustrated and angry.
I would get angry at myself. I would get angry at my mom for making me try to read.

I would throw temper tantrums too.

I also got pretty frustrated when my younger sister in first grade started correcting me when I read out loud. She was already a better reader than I was.

I struggled so much, I started to pretend to read-just faked it. I would even get silly and make up words.

In school, I would read the first letter of a word and make a guess. Instead of <u>smile</u> I would say <u>smell</u>.
I would read "I smell at my friend, Robert."
How embarrassing!!

Because it took me forever to read a sentence, my classmates would finish it for me sometimes.

I would get so tired. Doing twenty minutes of homework could take me two hours.

Most of that was just messing around to delay reading. I had a tough time concentrating.

Reading one page could take forever and I'd lose interest . . . and get way too distracted. A speck on the carpet would become fascinating and I was gone, off in my own little world.

Of course, the harder it got, the more I hated to read. The more I hated to read, the more I hated school.

I would start on Sunday saying that I didn't want to go to school that week.
I would argue with my mom every morning about going to school. All to avoid reading.
WHY couldn't I read?!

We finally went to an eye doctor who specializes in kids with difficulty reading. The doctor made me take a bunch of looooonnngggg tests. After taking all those tests, we found out that I have a special learning disability.

Why can't I read? We finally knew.

I have DYSLEXIA, which means 'difficulty understanding written or printed symbols.' Letters and numbers are symbols!

Well, the mystery was solved.
Now, what to do about it?

At school I get
special accommodations. I never have
to read out loud, unless I want to.
I get extra time on tests. I do my reading
with audio books. I only have to answer
the odd numbered questions on homework,
so it doesn't take me all night. I even get
to dictate my answers to my teachers.

At least people know more about dyslexia these days and my parents are getting me the right help.

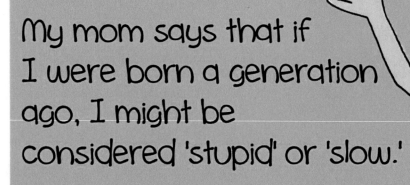

My mom says that if I were born a generation ago, I might be considered 'stupid' or 'slow.'

Today, people understand that kids like me can be as smart–or even smarter than–everyone else.

We can get special accommodations to make learning easier for us–to help our brains understand things better.

I'm also in really good company.

Do you know how many geniuses and great inventors are dyslexic?

Thomas Edison, Albert Einstein, Leonardo da Vinci, Alexander Graham Bell, Charles Schwab, Walt Disney, and William Hewlett! Some of the smartest minds in history! It's a pretty cool club.

13

I know I'll have to deal with my dyslexia my whole life, and I know that I have to learn to work around it.

Even though it may get easier, it will never be 'fixed.'

You know why?

Because I'm not broken!

Dyslexia Resources:

The National Center for Learning Disabilities:
http://www.ncld.org/

Bookshare: https://www.bookshare.org/

Dyslexia Help at the University of Michigan:
http://dyslexiahelp.umich.edu/

The International Dyslexia Association:
http://www.interdys.org/

24004051R00015

Made in the USA
Middletown, DE
10 September 2015